Festivals

My Chinese New Year

Monica Hughes

Raintree

Little Nippers

www.raintreepublishers.co.uk
Visit our website to find out
more information about
Raintree books.

To order:
☎ Phone 0845 6044371
🖨 Fax +44 (0) 1865 312263
📧 Email myorders@raintreepublishers.co.uk

Customers from outside the UK please telephone +44 1865 312262

Raintree is an imprint of Capstone Global Library Limited, a company incorporated in England and Wales having its registered office at 7 Pilgrim Street, London, EC4V 6LB – Registered company number: 6695582

Text © Capstone Global Library Limited 2005
First published in paperback in 2005
The moral rights of the proprietor have been asserted.

Editorial: Sarah Eason and Louise Galpine
Design: Jo Hinton-Malivoire and Tokay, Bicester, UK (www.tokay.co.uk)
Picture Research: Ruth Blair
Production: Severine Ribierre

Originated by Dot Gradations Ltd
Printed and bound in China by South China Printing Company

ISBN 0 431 16263 8 (hardback)
09 08 07 06 05
10 9 8 7 6 5 4 3 2 1

ISBN 978 1 406 24886 9 (paperback)
15 14 13 12
10 9

British Library Cataloguing in Publication Data
Hughes, Monica
Little Nippers Festivals My Chinese New Year

A full catalogue record for this book is available from the British Library.

Acknowledgements
The Publishers would like to thank the following for permission to reproduce photographs:
Alain Evrard/Lonely Planet Images p. **20**; TRIP pp. **21** (A Tory), **23** (H Rogers); all other pictures Harcourt Education/Tudor Photography.

Cover photograph of a celebration meal, reproduced with permission of Harcourt Education/Tudor Photography.

The Publishers would like to thank Philip Emmett for his assistance in the preparation of this book.

Every effort has been made to contact copyright holders of any material reproduced in this book. Any omissions will be rectified in subsequent printings if notice is given to the Publishers.

Contents

At school

I was born in the year of the tiger, so I'm making a tiger mask.

We all like the story of the twelve animals **racing** to decide each year's name.

5

Getting ready

Snip!

Snip!

I'm having my hair cut - it **tickles**!

My sister helps with all the **cleaning** and **polishing**.

Decorations

I love putting up the decorations outside.

We like to decorate inside the house, too.

9

Lots to prepare

Mmm! Doesn't this look good?

Looking our best

My sisters take a long time to get ready.

Perfect!

Now we are all going to see the rest of my family.

13

Our family meal

Mmm!

What shall I eat first?

Presents and cards

I wonder who sent this card.

What will be inside
my lucky envelope?

Games

New Year is a **lucky** time to play games.

This computer game
is **really** fun!

Dancing in the street

Everyone enjoys watching
the dragon dancers.

Fireworks

Mum says the firecrackers were very, very **noisy** when she was little.

Index

The end

Notes for adults

Most festivals and celebrations share common elements that will be familiar to the young child, such as new clothes, special food, sending and receiving cards and presents, giving to charity, being with family and friends and a busy and exciting build-up time. It is important that the child has an opportunity to compare and contrast their own experiences with those of the children in the book.

The following Early Learning Goals are relevant to this series:

Knowledge and understanding of the world
- Early learning goals for exploration and investigation: Discuss events that occur regularly within the children's experience, for example seasonal patterns, daily routines, celebrations

Personal, social and emotional development
- Early learning goals for a sense of community
- Respond to significant experiences, showing a range of feelings when appropriate
- Have a developing respect for their own cultures and beliefs and those of other people

Chinese people throughout the world celebrate the New Year for 15 days in January or February. Each New Year is named after one of twelve animals. It is thought unlucky to use scissors during the festival and so everyone visits the hairdresser or barber well before Chinese New Year. Families gather together and homes are 'spring cleaned' and decorated. Scrolls are put up outside the house to frighten 'bad spirits' and bring prosperity to the household. Special food is prepared and enjoyed. Everyone wears their smartest clothes and children are given lucky red and gold envelopes containing money. Traditional games are played at this lucky time of the year. Celebrations also take place in the street. Crowds gather to watch magnificent Lion and Dragon Dances and watch firework displays originally intended to frighten away anything 'evil'.